YOUR CHURCH IS NEWS

YOUR CHURCH IS NEWS

Raymond G. Mecca

JUDSON PRESS, VALLEY FORGE

YOUR CHURCH IS NEWS

Copyright © 1975
Judson Press, Valley Forge, PA 19481

Unless otherwise indicated, Bible quotations in this volume are in
accordance with the Revised Standard Version of the Bible, copyrighted
1952 and 1971 by the Division of Christian Education of the National
Council of the Churches of Christ in the United States of America, and are
used by permission.

Library of Congress Cataloging in Publication Data

Mecca, Raymond G.
  Your church is news.

   1. Church publicity.   I. Title.
 BV653.M4   254.4   75-9655
 ISBN 0-8170-0670-2

Printed in the U.S.A.   ⊕

To Phyllis

Contents

Introduction
Good News!

Early in his ministry, Jesus told those who wanted to keep him to themselves: "'I must preach the good news of the kingdom of God to the other cities also; for I was sent for this purpose'" (Luke 4:43).

Following his example and under the charge of the Great Commission, Christians have been telling the Good News of the gospel ever since.

Besides employing such methods as preaching and individual witnessing, the churches have made various other efforts as the task has become more complex in an increasingly pluralistic society.

Through the scheduling of activities for all kinds of people to meet all kinds of needs, churches preach a concerned Christ. Through involvement in the issues and problems of our times, they preach a universal Christ. Through ministries to people in all walks and stations of life, they preach a living, loving Christ.

But beyond the churches' direct efforts, today's world provides other means of communication. Through these, the churches can acquaint the uncommitted—those outside the normal channels of church communication—with the activities, projects, involvements, and people that in themselves present the Christ who reaches out to all.

After all, in the apostle Paul's words: "How are men to call upon him in whom they have not believed? And how are they to believe in him of whom they have never heard?" (Romans 10:14).

The media—newspapers, radio, and television—are available channels of communication. They perform this function willingly because their primary job is to acquaint people with the world around them, to present truth so that people can make realistic judgments as members of society.

The one limitation on this willingness, of course, is that the media are under obligation to give all sides a fair hearing and are thus reluctant to present sectarian points of view except as expressed by figures of note in public address.

To the media, events and people are news insofar as they interest or affect the lives of more than a select group. And, within that definition, the events and people of your church can be, and often are, news. Unfortunately, however, in many churches, they are not always so identified, and thus opportunities to use the important help of the media are lost.

This book is intended to help you recognize what and who can be considered newsworthy in your church and assist you in using the media in the most effective way to make the news known.

It will seek to help you enlist the interest and cooperation of editors so that the news will be published or broadcast.

And it will give you some guidelines to help attract the readers and listeners you want to reach and, ultimately, tell the best news of all: the Good News!

#

1 | Your Church Is News!

News is what's happening and who is making it happen in the world around us. It's people and things, ideas and events, nature and technology, groups and individuals.

The means by which we learn about what's happening and who's making it happen are the news media. These range from the major metropolitan newspaper which tells us of events in Europe, Asia, and the Middle East to the neighborhood gossip who relates a choice tidbit about the family up the street.

The media find out what's happening and who's making it happen through news sources.

The gossip's sources are usually neighbors whose reports are filtered through lively imaginations and inclinations to suspect the worst.

The newspaper's or broadcast station's sources may also be "neighbors"—witnesses to an event, persons acquainted with someone who's done something newsworthy, records and data relating to something or someone of general

NEWS IS WHAT'S HAPPENING and who's making it happen. News is tragedy and joy, inspiration and frustration, the power of evil and the triumph of good. A disastrous church fire is news, but news is also a group of young people giving of their time and effort to improve the environment by cleaning up a local stream. Your church is news—who will tell its story of service and commitment?

interest. These are sources whose reports are filtered through a detailed checking apparatus and a determination to get at the truth.

But the professional media's primary sources are the newsmakers themselves: the people, the groups, and the events that are sufficiently unusual or important and of wide enough interest to justify their reporting.

As an important organized group in your community, involving many people and touching the lives of even more, your church is news.

Fire Destroys
Zion Church
in Meadville

Vandals Mar Classrooms
at Wakefield Church

Yes, your church is news. But its newsworthiness is certainly not limited to its involvement in events of the type described in the headlines above.

Editors are also interested—because their readers are interested—in what positive things are happening at your church. Despite this, they frequently receive calls from church folk that start something like this:

"Hello, news desk."

"Hello. This is Mrs. Brown at Trinity Church. I know

you're mainly interested in news about murders and wars and scandals, but. . . ."

Nothing could be farther from the truth, because truth is what editors are interested in, the truth about the world we live in.

Now, a part of that truth is murder and war and scandal. To deny this is to deny reality and to live in a fantasy world where there are no tragedies, no evil, no problems. Recognizing these in the press, furthermore, not only draws attention to them, but also can prompt people to action, to seek cures for the world's ills.

Therefore, it would be wrong for the press to ignore the evil in society. At the same time, ignoring the events and people that are sources of hope, inspiration, and good example would promote an equal distortion of the truth.

Of course, it is obvious that the press cannot tell all that happens. Thus, its columns and broadcast time must be limited to the unusual and to news of widest interest.

Therefore, it may appear that a disproportionate amount of space and time is given, for instance, to crime and politics. Attention is given to crime, for example, because it is unusual; however, for every crime reported, there are myriad other acts of honesty and compassion that go unreported simply because they are so common. Attention is given to politics because they affect so many people, and the press has a unique role in acting as the public's watchdog on those who purport to serve the public.

An objective scanning of your local newspaper, however,

will disclose that a large portion of its columns are devoted to what we might call "news on the plus side." Likewise, considering quasi-news programs (like talk shows and documentaries) as well as regular news broadcasts, the same is true of radio and television.

In summary, then, editors are interested in presenting news on the plus side of truth's ledger. But, because of time and space limitations, it should be of relatively wide interest and sufficiently unusual to be worthy of note.

What specifically fits these criteria is a matter of largely subjective judgment. Churches may legitimately submit any news they believe worthy of public note. But don't be too disappointed if the editor occasionally disagrees.

Now, what could make your church newsworthy, short of mayhem or tragedy?

Well, starting at the beginning, your church is news when it's first organized.

The Church Begins

In any community, a church is recognized as an important institution, one which can be a vital force in a neighborhood's development.

A church is a fellowship of interest not only to its members, but also to others in the community. These others could be potential members or persons interested in a particular program or individual.

Therefore, the establishment of a church is a newsworthy event in a community. The media ought to be made aware of its establishment and be made acquainted with its leadership and with the details of its program.

The following news release is an example of one that might be submitted to local editors when a church is established:

Trinity Church

18 Elm Street, Millville, New York

NEWS RELEASE

For release: Immediately   Date: March 6, 19__

For further information, contact: Mrs. Vernon Sawyer
1221 Spruce Lane,
Millville, N.Y.
Bellview 4-3185

Under the auspices of (denominational group), a group of Millville residents will begin regular worship services Sunday, March 12.

The group is preparing a charter and looks forward to the early establishment of Trinity Church of Millville.

Rev. Barry Edwards, a visiting pastor from the National Board of Missions, is assisting the group and will conduct the worship services. William Smith of 312 Forest Drive, Millville, has been elected presiding officer.

Initially, Sunday services will be held at the Smith home. Persons interested in joining the fellowship have been invited to attend the services or contact Smith at Bellview 4-2817.

#

As the church organization progresses, there will be other newsworthy occasions. For instance:

—Adoption of the charter
—Changes in place or time of services
—Periodic progress reports
—Special speakers, programs, and new services
—Purchase of building site and building plans

The Church Celebrates

There are many occasions in the life of a church that are newsworthy. For example, an anniversary might provide an opportunity for several different news releases.

First, there would be the announcement of the anniversary and plans for its celebration. Consider the following example:

Trinity Church

18 Elm Street, Millville, New York

NEWS RELEASE

For release: Thursday, September 5

Date: August 27, 19—

For further information, contact: Mrs. Vernon Sawyer
1221 Spruce Lane,
Millville, N.Y.
Bellview 4-3185

Trinity Church, Millville, will inaugurate a year-long celebration of its tenth anniversary on Sunday, September

15, at its 11 A.M. worship service.

Special guest speaker will be Dr. Norman Wilkerson, who served as the church's first full-time pastor, from 1964 to 1970. He is currently a consultant to the National Board of Missions.

"We are pleased and honored to have Dr. Wilkerson return for this occasion," said the church's current pastor, Rev. William Desmond. "We look forward to his coming and to the many special events the congregation is planning for our anniversary year."

Trinity Church is located at 18 Elm St. It was officially chartered on (brief history).

Other events planned for the anniversary year include (upcoming events).

#

Also, interviews with notable people in the church's past might be of interest to editors or perhaps to radio and television talk-show hosts. These might include charter members, former pastors, or others.

Then, too, each separate event planned for the anniversary year should be announced by news release. When appropriate, pictures illustrating the church's past and present should be offered to editors for consideration (see chapter 8).

Editors might also consider use of a history of the church, especially if its role in the community has been a significant one and thus would be of wide interest.

The Church Builds

Church building programs are among the most

newsworthy aspects of church life. They affect a community both socially and economically. Their announcement helps a newspaper or broadcast station explain what's going on:

"What's happening at Front and Elm, Fred?"

"Well, John, I read in the *Gazette* that. . . ."

And building programs are of interest to nearly everyone in the community: churchmen and tradesmen, town leaders and the man on the street, the curious and the involved.

Again, more than one news release will be involved and there can be a number of related news opportunities.

Each major event in the process deserves announcement in some detail:

—Decision to build
—Choice of architect
—Design (make available to the press architect's sketch of how the new building will look)
—Selection of contractor
—Cost estimates and construction timetable
—Interesting (and often photogenic) events as construction progresses
—Building completion and plans for dedication
—Dedication services

If the church's new building is to have particularly interesting or unusually symbolic design or features, these might form the basis of a news release or interview by a reporter with the architect, building chairman, pastor, or the like.

A typical news release might read as follows:

Trinity Church
18 Elm Street, Millville, New York

NEWS RELEASE

For Release: Sunday, October 10, or thereafter

Date: October 7, 19—

For further information, contact: Mrs. Vernon Sawyer
1221 Spruce Lane,
Millville, N.Y.
Bellview 4-3185

Trinity Church, Millville, today (October 10) announced plans to construct a major addition to the church building at 18 Elm St.

The addition, a two-story wing, will house classrooms for the church school, a multipurpose room, church office, and pastor's study, according to Oscar DePaul, building chairman.

Architect for the project will be Lane Associates of 104 Main St., Millville.

De Paul said it is hoped that drawings can be submitted for congregational approval by December 10 and that construction can begin next year.

Harold Martin of 1328 Springdale Ave., Millville, has been named building fund chairman.

The church's present facility, built in 1965, includes a sanctuary (presently convertible into a multipurpose room), church office, and four classrooms. The congregation numbers 375.

"We've just outgrown our present building," said the church's pastor, Rev. William Desmond. "The new addition will enable us to serve better a growing congregation and better meet the needs of our community."

#

Also, announcement of and progress reports on the building fund campaign would be newsworthy.

The Church Gives

A congregation's stewardship is news. It is of wide interest as a manifestation of what we might call the "philanthropy phenomenon," that is, America's propensity for giving to charitable causes.

Announcement of the stewardship campaign, its goal, and leadership, can form the basis for a news release. So, too, can announcement of any planned canvassing.

"Who are those people out ringing doorbells, Fred?"

"Well, John, I read in the *Gazette* that. . . ."

And then, of course, there needs to be announcement of the campaign's actual achievement in pledges.

The above would apply also to specific campaigns such as those conducted for missions or other special causes.

Additional news opportunities in your church will be illustrated in succeeding chapters. The list in this book, however, is far from exhaustive. It is intended to affirm what editors know and what more church people need to realize:

YOUR CHURCH IS NEWS!

#

2 | Events Are News!

Consider the following reports which might have appeared in two newspapers telling of the same event.

The first item is an example of how the Lenten series might have been reported in a major metropolitan daily in the city of which Millville is a suburb.

Lenten Services Set at Millville Church

The annual interdenominational series of Lenten services in Millville will be held this year at Trinity Church, 18 Elm St., beginning this Wednesday.

Guest speakers will include ministers from various Millville churches. At the initial service, Rev. Willard Bell of St. Luke's Church will speak on the topic, "Our Lenten Pilgrimage."

The services, to be held each Wednesday at 7 P.M. through April 3, will also feature special music by adult, youth, and children's choirs.

\#

The second illustrates how the series might be reported in the weekly Millville newspaper.

Trinity Church to Host
Millville Lenten Series

The annual interdenominational series of Lenten services in Millville will be held this year at Trinity Church, 18 Elm St.

The services will be held each Wednesday evening at 7 P.M. beginning this week and continuing through April 3.

They will be under the general sponsorship of the Millville Ministerium and will feature Lenten messages by clergymen from various churches in the Millville area.

A special highlight of this year's series will be anthems sung by choirs from participating churches on the series theme, "The Way to the Cross."

This week, the speaker will be Rev. Willard Bell of St. Luke's Church, Main and Court Sts., Millville. Dr. Bell's topic will be, "Our Lenten Pilgrimage." Special music will be provided by the adult and children's choirs of St. Luke's Church.

The schedule for succeeding weeks includes:

(continues with listing of upcoming events)

#

On a local radio station, the item might have been heard on a program called "Community Calendar" as follows:

Churches in the Millville area will open a series of Lenten services this week. The services will be held each Wednesday at 7 P.M. at Trinity Church, 18 Elm St. Various Millville

ministers will speak at the services, and there will be special
music by adult and junior choirs. For further information,
contact Trinity Church at Bellview 4-1050.

All of these reports would have been based on the same
news release from the church. But each editor adapted it to
his format and, more importantly, to his constituency's
interests and makeup.

Note that all thought the series newsworthy. This illustrates the fact that events in your church are worth
bringing to the attention of the media, both local and
metropolitan.

Sometimes the editor will have to reject an item for lack of
space or time available. But events in your church are
newsworthy. And if your concern that people know what
your church is offering extends beyond the bounds of your
congregation, use the news release to send out the word to
the media.

What kinds of events are reportable? They fall into
categories that reflect your church program. A discussion of
several of these categories follows.

Worship

Some newspapers carry announcements of sermon topics
and hours of services and other programs as part of a weekly
church calendar. If one of your local papers does this, ask the
editor how this information is to be submitted, then put this
on your calendar as a weekly responsibility.

Special services deserve special note. Supply editors with a more detailed news release if, for instance, a special speaker is planned. Provide biographical data on the speaker and also any information on the particular occasion for his or her appearance.

Unique worship services should be reported. For instance, if a folk mass is scheduled or if a lay group in the church is to conduct the service in a special way, let the public know via the press.

Series of services for particular seasons or other occasions are newsworthy, especially, as in the example with which this chapter began, if more than one church is involved.

Some churches have special musical services featuring choirs, organists, soloists, instrumentalists, etc. These should be the subjects of separate news releases, and the announcements should give complete information including music to be performed.

If several special occasions are scheduled over a relatively short period of time, you might provide the editors with both a comprehensive news release as well as an individual release covering each upcoming event.

Each of the special occasions listed in the comprehensive release should be the subject of a separate announcement to the media:

—The three musical programs

—The midweek Lenten services

—The March 23 missions service

—The fund-raising campaign and its results

An example of a comprehensive news release might be as follows:

Trinity Church

18 Elm Street, Millville, New York

NEWS RELEASE

For release: Thursday, February 27

Date: February 18, 19—

For further information, contact: Mrs. Vernon Sawyer
1221 Spruce Lane,
Millville, N.Y.
Bellview 4-3185

The month of March will bring a number of special services to Trinity Church, 18 Elm St., Millville.

As part of its Lenten observance, the church will present special Sunday evening musical programs at 7 P.M. on March 2, 16, and 30.

This Sunday evening, the senior choir will present. . . . On March 16, the "Singing Troubadors" of. . . . On March 30, the youth choir will be featured as part of a service to be conducted by the church's youth fellowship.

The special midweek Lenten services will continue at 7 P.M. Wednesdays with pastors of various Millville churches preaching. Those participating in March will be. . . .

On March 23, Dr. Harold Manor, president of Christian College, Lakeland, Michigan, will preach at the 11 A.M. service. Dr. Manor will speak on the topic, "Christian Mission in a Changing World."

Also during the month of March, the church is conducting a special fund-raising campaign to purchase a new piano for the church school. Announcement of the campaign's results will be made at the 11 A.M. service on March 30.

#

Depending on the publication day of your local newspaper (if it's not a daily), mark the releases to be published a few days in advance of each event. For instance, the missions service announcement might be marked: "For release: March 18."

Other series of services—evangelistic, missionary, etc.—are also newsworthy. If they involve guest speakers or musicians, include biographical sketches with, or as part of, your news release.

Programs

The variety of programs in a typical church's calendar precludes any exhaustive list of news opportunities here. But a few examples will suffice to show the kinds of programs editors will be interested in reporting in their news columns and on the air.

In general, the public press is interested only in public events, that is, programs open to the public. This means that a congregational dinner or business meeting limited in attendance to the membership of the church is not ordinarily of news value unless, of course, something unusual occurs that would be of wider interest. This would usually hold true also for church committee, board, or council meetings.

On the other hand, if a program open to the public is planned, for instance, to follow a dinner, then this would be a legitimate subject for a news announcement.

If advance registration or reservations are required for participation in an event, or if a charge for attendance is involved, this should be noted in the news release.

Vacation church schools are a good example of the kind of church program that is of special interest to editors. This is true not only because they affect a wider number of families than some other church programs, but also because they often provide opportunities for pictures (see chapter 8).

Groups sponsored by the church often have special programs that might be newsworthy—from the couples' club's upcoming splash party to the scout troop's court of honor, from the men's fellowship's breakfast to the youth group's hay ride—all are reportable, assuming they are open to the public.

Remember that if the event is not open, but the event is announced in the public press, the limitation on attendance should be noted in the release.

Special Events

One of the most significant special events in the life of a church is the arrival of a new pastor. Most congregations schedule special receptions in his honor, one of the purposes of which is to acquaint him with church members and community leaders and them with him.

Although news opportunities in connection with the pastor will be discussed in more detail in chapter 4, the receptions are noted here as events to be announced.

The dedication of a new church building or addition is likewise newsworthy (see also chapter 1), as are dinners, banquets, sports events, topical programs, outings, etc., to which the public is invited.

Breaking News

Thus far, our emphasis has been on announcement of upcoming events. These kinds of announcements will form the bulk of news the church produces.

However, there will also be occasions when something newsworthy happens at the church and should be reported after it happens.

Examples would be: the calling of a pastor, the announcement of a stewardship campaign's results, and remarks of a qualified person on matters of community interest.

If details are known in advance (such as in the case of a tabulated pledge total) but are to be announced publicly at a special time, inform the editor via an appropriate "For Release" date to coincide with the announcement.

If details are not known until the event takes place, but something newsworthy is expected to occur, contact the editor and either arrange with him for a reporter to attend or for you to get the information to him after the event takes place.

Of course, newsworthy occurrences cannot always be

predicted! For this reason, it is good to have established a relationship with editors of local newspapers and broadcast stations and to know how to reach them in case news breaks and contact must be made quickly.

The following sequence may serve as an example:

September 15—A town councilman agrees to speak at a Laymen's Sunday service at your church on October 12.

September 20—News release sent out to local newspapers and broadcast stations announcing the Laymen's Sunday program.

October 5 and 6—Vandals damage two local churches and several homes.

October 7—Five young people arrested in connection with vandalism. Incidents and police action arouse community concern.

October 9—Councilmen plan meeting with residents for October 13.

October 10—You contact local editors to ask about coverage of councilman's address on Sunday. Councilman informs the press he plans no major announcement, but may touch on problem of delinquency "from a Christian point of view." Editor of local newspaper arranges to have reporter present for councilman's Laymen's Sunday address. Other editors will have reporters contact councilman and you after the service for report. Local radio station arranges to tape record councilman's remarks for possible rebroadcast or use of excerpts in news programs.

In this example, you, as church news director, served both the church, in letting people know of its community concern in originally scheduling the speaker, and the public, by informing the press of a possibly significant news event. Also, in encouraging the reporting of remarks that would give a Christian perspective on a community issue, you served the Christian mission as well.

Note that if the speaker had been the pastor, this would not have been of so great an interest to the media; not because his views would be any less relevant or insightful, but because he would not have the qualification of direct involvement that the councilman has.

From the media's point of view, a person's comments on an issue are newsworthy in direct proportion to his direct involvement or personal qualifications to speak on the issue at hand.

In summary, editors are interested—because their readers are—in the events taking place at your church. Their needs, space, and time available may vary, but public worship services, programs, and special events should be fully reported to them. Be sure news releases are in their hands well in advance of release dates to permit them maximum time and flexibility in using the information. And be sure to let editors know if any important or unusual events are expected or have just taken place.

Do this with confidence, because editors agree with you:

EVENTS ARE NEWS!

#

3 | Projects Are News!

Churches undertake many projects in the process of maintaining their programs and serving their communities.

News editors are interested in church projects because they involve people at work, giving of themselves and their talents, often touching the lives of people beyond the immediate congregation.

Church Forms Corporation to Build Housing for Needy

Youth at St. Peter's Plan Glass Recycling

Bethel Group Offers to Help Tutor Pupils

Yes, projects, large and small, are news. Let's think about what newsworthy projects, categorized by groups involved, might be found in the typical church.

Youth Group Projects

Young people are very project-oriented. They are concerned about the church and the world they live in and have energy to spare. Put these two characteristics together and you realize why the most successful youth fellowships are the most active in serving church and community.

More and more, with the increasing awareness of the myriad threats to our environment, young people are ecologically aware.

Consider the following example of a possible news release:

Trinity Church

18 Elm Street, Millville, N. Y.

NEWS RELEASE

For release: Immediately   Date: April 30, 19—

For further information, contact: Mrs. Vernon Sawyer
                                   1221 Spruce Lane,
                                   Millville, N.Y.
                                   Bellview 4-3185

The youth fellowship at Millville's Trinity Church is planning a stream cleanup project Saturday (May 5) at Valley Creek.

The creek has been the subject of numerous complaints by residents who say increasing trash and litter mar the creek's natural beauty.

The young people are planning their project to extend from the Court St. bridge to the foot of Elm St.

"We hope this will encourage other groups to take on similar projects," said David Walker of 132 Elm St., youth group president.

The group will meet at the church, 18 Elm St., at 8:30 A.M. Saturday. Accompanying them will be the pastor of Trinity Church, Rev. William Desmond, and Mr. and Mrs. Bruce Daley of 1326 Spruce Lane.

Other members of the congregation and community residents have been invited to assist in the project, Walker said.

Those participating will have a picnic lunch on the church grounds at noon. Each is asked to bring a box lunch with beverage to be provided by the church.

It is expected the project will be completed by 4:30 P.M.

Arrangements have been made to transport the collected litter by truck to the Millville landfill. Plastic collection bags will be provided.

If inclement weather postpones the project, it will be held the following Saturday (May 12) at the same time.

#

In addition to sending out the news release, the news director might personally contact editors at local television stations for possible coverage of the cleanup campaign by film crews. In addition to television film coverage for inclusion in a news program, newspaper editors might be interested in photographic coverage and should be contacted about this. However, since the local radio station is an aural medium it would probably not be interested in direct coverage.

This serves to illustrate the fact that in offering news to the media, the peculiar format of each medium should be considered.

Newspapers are a print and pictorial medium and consequently would have broader needs than television, a primarily pictorial medium. Radio, as an aural medium, calls for conciseness and simplicity of statement.

In many instances, various aspects of the same story will lend themselves best to different media. For example, the announcement in advance of the stream cleanup would lend itself best to print; an interview with the youth group president or pastor about the project would lend itself to radio; and the actual coverage of the event would lend itself to television.

These approaches are not mutually exclusive, of course. The interview might well be part of the advance announcement in the newspaper; the event might be covered photographically by the newspaper; the interview might be done on television; and the advance announcement might be carried on radio.

As news media, all are interested in reporting a story completely. But the peculiarities of each one's format may well dictate how each reports it.

Men's and Women's Group Projects

Although some laymen's groups gather primarily for a monthly breakfast or similar occasion with a guest speaker or program (newsworthy events in themselves), many of them undertake projects in service to the church or community.

Perhaps they may undertake a renovation project at the church: the nursery gets a needed repainting, the church school furniture is refurbished. Or they may participate in a project in evangelism: two-by-two visitation, for instance.

Then, too, they may choose a community service project: a tutoring program for slow learners at the neighborhood school or a rehabilitation effort in an economically depressed area.

These all are examples of projects that would be apt subjects for news releases, feature stories (see chapter 7), interviews, or coverage by the media.

Remember again that projects which are of wide community concern and relevance and involve visually interesting activities might well be subjects for television coverage or photos. Bring those kinds of opportunities to the special attention of editors, for the possibilities may be missed because of the sheer volume of releases that cross their desks.

Like the men's groups, women's fellowships often undertake projects that are of interest to the public. One example might be the following:

Trinity Church
18 Elm Street, Millville, N.Y.

NEWS RELEASE

For release: February 15   Date: February 10, 19—

For further information, contact: Mrs. Vernon Sawyer
1221 Spruce Lane,
Millville, N.Y.
Bellview 4-3185

The Women's Fellowship of Trinity Church, Millville, is planning a used-book sale for the benefit of the church building fund.

Donations of used books are being sought for the sale. It is scheduled for Saturday, March 10, from 10 A.M. to 5 P.M. at the church, 18 Elm St.

Arrangements for donations may be made by contacting the church office (Bellview 4-1050) or Mrs. Harold Martin, 1328 Springdale Ave., Millville (Bellview 4-7121).

"We are seeking donations of all kinds of books, fiction and nonfiction," said Mrs. Martin, Women's Fellowship president. "Both hardback and paperback books are welcome."

Proceeds of the sale will go toward furnishing a kindergarten classroom in the church wing now under construction, Mrs. Martin said.

#

Again, the wider the interest (in the above case, it is community-wide), the greater the likelihood an editor will find the item sufficiently newsworthy for him to use.

Also, the more unusual projects will command the greater attention: a bandage-rolling session for foreign missions, for instance, would be of somewhat less interest than a quilting bee to benefit a nearby home for the aged and infirm.

Also, a project with local relevance will be of greater interest to local readers and listeners and thus to local editors. The greater the local relevance, the greater the local interest and the more noteworthy it is in the local press.

Church Committee Projects

An active social-action committee is a ready source of project-type news stories. Also, an interview with its chairman regarding the church's approach to its social ministry as well as its plans for a given church year could well be of interest to newspapers or to a local talk-show host.

The board of Christian education also may have special projects scheduled in connection with church school outreach programs or special efforts outside the normal curriculum schedule, such as a nursery school or day-care center.

Summer camping projects, especially if they involve youngsters and adults outside the immediate congregation, are certainly newsworthy. They will provide advance announcement releases, human interest stories as camp progresses, and picture (newspaper or television) opportunities.

The church news director might profitably plan to spend a

day at the camp, talking with counselors and campers. Interesting or unusual activities and humorous anecdotes could well be of interest in the local press.

Recently, a parent called the editor of a metropolitan newspaper to report that two youngsters were starting a seesaw-a-thon for charity. They secured pledges for every hour they kept seesawing. They lasted forty-four hours, and the phone call resulted in a heartwarming story with pictures. Similar human interest stories can be found at most summer camps.

People involved in interesting and beneficial activities are newsworthy. Your church has many examples of these, and nearly all, you'll find, are of interest not only to you and your congregation, but to others in your community as well, because

PROJECTS ARE NEWS!

#

4 | People Are News!

You will find that people can be the most productive sources of news in your church—not necessarily as members of groups or involved in events or projects, but as themselves.

Yet, people are the most often overlooked.

Church programs, events, and projects are to be publicized and reported; this is widely recognized. But people create this news through planning and execution. People are the ones who fashion them and carry them through. But the people are often lost in the publicizing or reporting of the programs.

Who are some of the people in your church who might be newsmakers?

The Pastor

We begin with the most obvious newsmaker in the church, the pastor.

As indicated in chapter 2, the pastor's arrival is an

important news event. So are his original calling and, subsequently, his resignation and departure.

Biographical data and appropriate pictures should be included with reports of these events to the media, but be sure that release dates reflect the timetable of congregational action and notification as well as church policy.

The pastor's activities, because of the very nature of his job, are largely in the public arena and thus are newsworthy. He preaches and conducts worship in public. He leads and participates in public events and programs. He offers a variety of services to the public. He probably serves in numerous public groups—civic and church related. Through his visitation and community involvement, he is aware of and probably knowledgeable about public issues.

Each of these activities can provide grist for the news mill operating at your church. Let's consider just a few of the possibilities.

Preaching

As was pointed out earlier, the media cannot, out of fairness to all, report purely sectarian statements. There are too many, first of all; also, they are limited in interest, and their diversity is too complex to be covered fairly.

One exception to this might be a major interchurch effort, such as those conducted by Billy Graham or other well-known evangelists. In such a case, the media will probably report the event and even portions of the message.

But most sermons do not generate the wide interest of such

an event and so are not generally given a place in the public press.

Some newspapers, however, do print a "Sermon of the Week." If your local newspaper has such a feature, and your pastor is not on the list of contributors, see if you can arrange to have him become one. Then arrange to have his messages transcribed so that some may be included in the series according to the newspaper's schedule.

There are occasions when a pastor's comments on a particular occasion—perhaps on an issue of local importance—may be of interest to local editors. Generally speaking, for his comments to be newsworthy he should be specially "qualified" in the subject, his comments should be relevant and insightful, and the media's scope should be considered.

The matters of relevance and insight are obviously important. As to that of "qualification," he should be specially equipped by training or experience to comment on the given subject.

For example, the average pastor's comments on the general state of the world economy would not be newsworthy in most editors' eyes. But his comments on ways to deal with a pocket of poverty near his church probably would be, assuming they speak to the issue and show reasoned insight.

Of course, the comments' newsworthiness depends on the scope of the newspaper or station involved. The one pastor in a small town would be more frequently quotable in the local newspaper than would the one pastor of hundreds in a metropolitan area on the city's network television station.

The same would hold true for the pastor's addresses before local groups: PTA's, civic organizations, service clubs, etc. Here, generally speaking, the sectarian aspect would not be an issue, but the criteria of qualification, relevance and insight, and scope still apply.

If an advance text of a sermon or address is available, use this as a basis for your news release. But be sure to mark it for release after the actual speaking time and be sure to let editors know if he digresses from or significantly alters the prepared text in delivery.

If no prepared text is available, arrange to tape-record the sermon or address to be sure you are accurate in quoting the speaker.

Leading

As program leader in the church, or at least as active planner and participant in most church programs, the pastor is eminently qualified to speak of the purpose and expectations as well as of details of events in his church. If the events are of sufficiently wide interest and import, he might also be quotable in the media as an evaluator of a program after it is completed.

Catching up what was said in previous chapters and adding this, we can see how an event like a vacation church school might provide at least three news opportunities:

—Before the event: announcement of the school and details about it.

—During the event: reports of human interest sidelights or unusual activities, including pictures.

—After the event: results (attendance, accomplishments, etc.), evaluation, and plans for the future as viewed by the pastor.

Serving

The pastor serves the community in many ways: on local boards and committees, through visitation and counseling, as well as through personal contact with community leaders.

He does this not for publicity, but out of a sense of concern and calling in the servant ministry. But there will undoubtedly be occasions when his social involvement may qualify him to speak out on public issues.

If he plans a public address on a given subject, this, of course, can be reported as suggested above. If, on the other hand, his comments are not to be part of an address or sermon, use an interview technique in reporting his views.

In preparing for an interview, list all questions you can think of as pertinent to the subject. From among these, choose certain priority questions you see as essential to getting the person interviewed to speak relevantly on the subject at hand.

Unless you are equipped to take shorthand (the standard type or one of your own devising), arrange to tape-record the interview. An inexpensive cassette recorder will serve this purpose well and would be a handy tool for you in recording other interviews and even speeches or sermons.

During the interview, listen to the person being interviewed. Don't make the mistake of thinking about your next question as the person answers the previous one. What the person says may well suggest better questions than those you have prepared in advance. But try to be sure the person answers all your "priority" questions.

In writing a report of the interview, periodically break up the quotations with paraphrases or information about the person interviewed or the subject matter. Also, relate the quotations beginning with the most important and group them as best you can by topic. Little or no attention need be paid to the chronological sequence of the actual interview except where this is essential to the meaning of what was said.

Consider the following typical interview report:

Trinity Church

18 Elm Street, Millville, New York

NEWS RELEASE

For Release: Immediately   Date: October 14, 19—

For further information, contact: Mrs. Vernon Sawyer
1221 Spruce Lane,
Millville, N.Y.
Bellview 4-3185

An end to the outbreak of vandalism in Millville early this week will depend on the close cooperation of police, parents, youth, school, and community leaders.

That is the view of Rev. William Desmond, pastor of Trinity Church, Millville, and a member of the town council's newly formed public advisory committee.

"We have to act quickly and in concert if the problem is to be solved," Mr. Desmond said in an interview Tuesday (October 14).

Commenting on the arrests of five youths, aged 14 to 16, in connection with the vandalism, Mr. Desmond said:

"Arrests are not the whole answer. Certainly any wrongdoers must be apprehended and punished. But we also must answer our youth's need for additional recreational programs and facilities."

Mr. Desmond has been pastor of Trinity Church, 18 Elm St., for four years and was named to the council's advisory group at a public meeting Monday night.

"The committee is working urgently to bring adults and youth together to solve the immediate problem and seek answers to the long-range need," he said.

The committee met following Monday night's public meeting and plans to meet again soon, according to Mr. Desmond.

#

A transcript of the actual interview might have read as follows:

INTERVIEWER: Pastor, as a member of the town council's

new advisory committee, would you comment on the arrest of the five boys in connection with the vandalism in town this week?

PASTOR: Well, we'll have to see if these boys are, in fact, the ones involved, or the only ones. But, you know, arrests aren't the whole answer.

INTERVIEWER: What do you mean?

PASTOR: Well, there's . . . well, let me say first that certainly any wrongdoers must be apprehended and punished. But we also must answer our youth's need for additional recreational programs and facilities.

INTERVIEWER: What is being . . .

PASTOR: On the vandalism, though, we've got to get the police and parents working together as well as the school and community leaders. That's the only way we've got a chance to end it.

INTERVIEWER: These people have to work together?

PASTOR: Yes, and we have to act quickly and in concert if the problem is to be solved.

INTERVIEWER: Are the same groups going to have to work on the long-range recreation problem, too?

PASTOR: Yes, exactly, but the kids, too. Let's not forget the youth have to be involved. It can't be all from us to them. The committee is working urgently to bring adults and youth together to solve the immediate problem as well as to seek answers to the long-range need.

INTERVIEWER: Is the committee planning a meeting soon?

PASTOR: Well, you know . . . you were at the public session last night, weren't you?

INTERVIEWER: Yes, I was.

PASTOR: I thought I'd seen you there. Well, in any event, as you know we had a meeting afterward, and we met for a couple of hours, actually. As for the future, I expect we'll be meeting again very soon. I must get to the hospital for a visit now. I hope I've answered your questions.

INTERVIEWER: You have, pastor. Thanks for your time.

PASTOR: Thanks for your interest.

Church Members

Church members may, like the pastor, be qualified to comment on a specific event or issue. As laymen, they may also address the congregation or groups in it. Generally speaking, your coverage of them would be limited to their involvement in church programs or appearances before church groups.

The same general guidelines as given above for dealing with the pastor as newsmaker would also apply here.

Some church members may be interesting as subjects themselves, such as those who have done something unusual, or those who are marking an unusual occasion in their own or their families' lives.

View special anniversaries, trips, achievements, and public recognitions as news reporting opportunities in your congregation. See, for example, in chapter 7, the report on the ninety-year-old lady remembering her baptism in 1898.

Church Visitors

Special visitors to your church, coming to lead programs or preach, as well as those from far places or visiting for unusual reasons, are newsworthy.

Perhaps in addition to the news announcement of an upcoming event with a guest leader, an interview with the guest might make an appropriate supplementary article (known as a sidebar).

Most events in the church will involve interesting people, and sidebars about them are always appropriate. Because of space or time limitations, the main article and sidebar may wind up combined into one by the editor. But the final piece will probably be more interesting and readable as a result of the additional submission.

Although a sidebar is intended as a complement to the main article on an event, include basic information about the event in the sidebar as well. After all, the sidebar may be the only article some people may read or hear.

In summary, the pastor and members of and visitors to your congregation are interesting people. They often do interesting things and comment with qualification and insight on matters of public concern. No news is more widely read than that dealing with our fellows in the human family. For these reasons, always be conscious of the fact that

PEOPLE ARE NEWS!

#

5 | Gathering the News!

News media, large and small, share a common series of steps in performing their task. The larger and more complex the newspaper or broadcast station, the more individuals will be involved in the process. In smaller operations, fewer people will participate. But the steps are essentially the same:

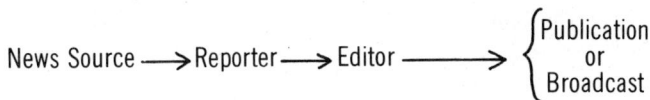

$$\text{News Source} \longrightarrow \text{Reporter} \longrightarrow \text{Editor} \longrightarrow \begin{cases} \text{Publication} \\ \text{or} \\ \text{Broadcast} \end{cases}$$

Until now, we have been discussing the sources of news in your church: programs, events, projects, and people.

We have referred to "editors" as those professionals at newspapers and radio and television stations who decide what news is to be published or broadcast.

In a sense, however, you, as church news director, are both a reporter and an editor; you observe the news source and relate the news, but also decide if it is sufficiently newsworthy to pass on to the media. You are also an editor in that you check over your news release for accuracy, completeness, and clarity of expression before you send them to the news media.

The larger your church, the more often you will find yourself in the role of editor, assigning others to report certain events or conduct particular interviews, asking others to submit data for news releases or to write them for you to pass on.

If yours is a small church, as in a small newspaper, you will find yourself often doing both the reporter's and the editor's job.

But even in small churches, one person can't possibly keep up with all the groups in the congregation, be aware of all their plans and projects, and be in vital touch with all the members.

For this reason, in order to help you do a successful job as church news director, you should organize a staff to help you.

Organizing Your Staff

Ask one reliable person on each of the church boards and committees to keep you informed of activities and projects which are planned, decisions which are made, and achievements which are noted.

In a large church, some of these contact persons may help you by preparing news releases regarding events and people on their "beat" (area of responsibility). If you are in a small church, you probably will do much of this yourself. But your contact persons can serve as your eyes and ears and also act as your liaisons with church groups to set up interviews or pictures.

Of course, once a news director grasps the potential for news, even in a small church, the job may be found too extensive for one person to handle efficiently. There may be time conflicts in events to be covered, in various deadlines to be met, as well as other conflicts.

Early on, then, find at least one or two other persons to help you cover the news in your church. Assign each a "beat," and take one yourself, as well. Encourage them to organize helpers—one contact person per board or group—as outlined above.

You also may want to secure the help of a qualified typist in the congregation to help in preparing news releases or articles for submission to the media.

Again, in small churches, one person can do the job with the help of board and group contact-persons. But the more people that are involved in news gathering in the church, the more news will be gathered.

Coverage will occasionally overlap: a building committee decision may involve another in church council; the pastor will be encountered on all three "beats." But the chart shown gives an idea of how responsibility for news gathering may be shared.

A typical news organization in the church might be as follows:

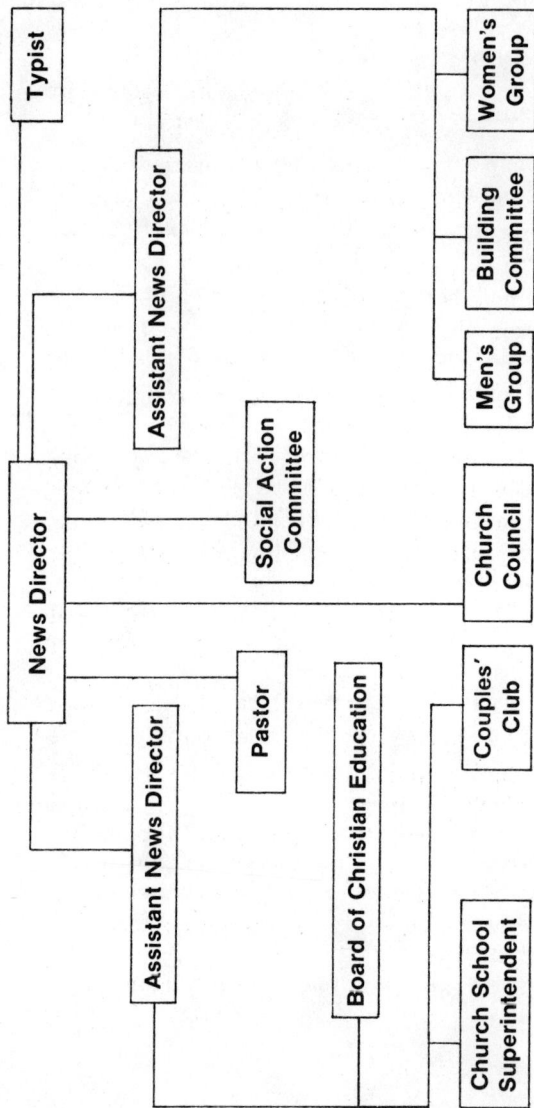

Sample Church News Organization

The chart shows the following structure:

- **News Director** (top level), connected to a **Typist**
- Under the News Director:
  - **Assistant News Director**
  - **Assistant News Director**
  - **Pastor**
  - **Social Action Committee**
- **Assistant News Director** connects to:
  - **Men's Group**
  - **Building Committee**
  - **Women's Group**
- **Church Council**
- **Board of Christian Education** connects to:
  - **Church School Superintendent**
  - **Couples' Club**

Training Your Staff

Secure copies of this manual for your assistants or encourage them to read yours. Use it to help build their enthusiasm for news gathering in your church. Meet with them to discuss how its suggestions can best be adapted to your church situation.

Once your assistants are sufficiently grounded in the task and challenged by its potential, organize a meeting of all contact persons.

If the group is large, divide it among yourself and your assistants. If it is relatively small, divide the leadership responsibility with your assistants, but remain as one group.

It would be helpful to have copies of this manual available for examination by the contact persons. They may want to use them during or after the training session. In any event, use it as resource material in preparing for the session.

A typical agenda for the training session might be as follows:

Opening prayer or worship	**pastor**
Introduction: "Our Church Is News"	**news director**
Events and Projects Are News	
	assistant news director
People Are News	**assistant news director**
How We'll Gather the News	**news director**

1. Put organization chart on board or newsprint.

2. Establish lines of communication and procedures for liaison.

3. **Stress awareness of and alertness to picture possibilities.**

Question/answer period   **all participants**
Closing remarks and summary
                              news director and assistants
Closing prayer or worship   **pastor**

If others than yourself or your assistants are to prepare news releases, you may want to set up a workshop using the material in chapters 6 and 7 of this manual as resource material.

One of the news media editors in your community might be willing to lead such a workshop or address your staff. Visits of the staff to local newspapers and broadcast stations can also be arranged with profit for all. Personal contacts of this type will prove invaluable as you and your staff carry on your tasks.

Set a Deadline Schedule

Through contact with local editors, make a list of their deadlines. Set up your own deadline schedule in advance of these to allow for news release preparation, transmission, and unforeseen delays.

For instance, if your local paper is a weekly and is published on Thursday, its deadline for church news may be as early as Monday. Material for that paper, then, should be submitted to you the preceding Thursday for preparation into news-release form and transmission to the paper.

Even for community calendar programs on radio or television, deadlines may be well in advance of a given day's program. Check with the station's program director or news editor and establish appropriate deadlines for your staff and yourself.

Also check with local editors about their deadlines for late-breaking news, in case you should need this information at any time.

Expanding the Staff

Word will eventually get around that the church is news and that someone's doing something about it. The larger your staff, the sooner and wider the word will spread.

Also take advantage of the regular means of church announcement to tell others of your interest in news. Remember that the more people you make aware of your interest and responsibility, the more potential for news sources becomes available to you.

The media: Your appointment as church news director is newsworthy in itself and should be reported to the media. Appointment of your assistants and staff is also worthwhile to submit.

The church bulletin: Your appointment and periodic reminders of your interests and responsibility should be noted in the Sunday church bulletin. This will keep the congregation aware of your desire for their help in learning of possible news or features.

The church newsletter: Here there will also be opportunity to report on the activities of you and your staff as well as to seek the help of the church membership in carrying out your responsibilities.

Pastoral announcement: At worship and at various meetings and programs, ask the pastor to encourage the congregation to be aware of the church as news. Work closely with the pastor, possibly arranging regular meetings with him to discuss news possibilities. Of all church members, he is probably your best contact person because of his involvement in the whole church program and in the interest he shares with you in reporting news from the church to the public.

Displays and Exhibits: Keep a personal file of clippings from the press regarding your church. Display these from time to time to keep the congregation aware that your church is news.

Speakers and Programs: Encourage church groups to invite local media representatives to speak or participate in programs, workshops, and the like. As with your staff, congregational contact with these persons will help encourage the awareness of news reporting as an important church activity.

With the help of pastor, assistants, and contact persons, as well as the added enthusiasm generated in the congregation, you'll find it more and more exhilarating to be involved in

GATHERING THE NEWS!

#

6 | Telling the News!

Now that we've discovered what can make news in your church, let's turn to the "nitty-gritty" of putting that news into a form that the media will use.

The first thing to keep in mind is that editors agree that your church's events and people are news. They're on your side.

The editor is not printing or broadcasting your church's news as a favor. He realizes that it is of interest to the people who read his newspaper or listen to his station. And he's anxious to present what's of interest to those people.

But remember, too, that there are many other events and people in the world making news. In choosing what he will publish or broadcast, the editor must often make a choice between various pieces of news because his space and broadcast time are limited.

He's also a very busy person. Few people realize the volume of newsworthy items that comes to the average editor's attention. This is most true of those who are responsible for copy on a metropolitan newspaper or radio/television station. But it applies, as well, to those who work on small weekly papers.

To better acquaint yourself with an editor's work, plan to tour a local newspaper or station. If you have a smaller paper or radio station nearby, it might be possible for you to talk to the editor personally.

One of the most frequent kinds of phone calls received by an editor is the one from a newly appointed publicity chairman of a church organization. The question asked of the editor can be summarized as follows: "What information do I need to provide for you to publish (broadcast) my news?" The answer is really six answers because there are six basic answers that every well-reported news story must give, no matter how long or short:

Who? Whom is the news about and whom does it affect?

What? What happened or is being announced?

When? When did or will the event or experience happen?

Where? Where did or will it take place and from where did the people involved come? Be as specific as possible. Editors prefer that you include exact addresses to aid the reader or listener and also because the editor may need to check with one or more of the persons involved. If you wish exact addresses omitted from the published account, you should indicate it.

How? How did the event come about? How did the person involved come to have his or her experience? What is the meaning of the news in the perspective of related matters?

Why? Why is the event being held? Why is the person's experience unique? What makes the person interesting outside his or her normal level of acquaintance?

Those are the six basic questions that should be answered in any well-reported news story. They should be answered in your "news release."

Preparing the News Release

A news release is a written disclosure of news.

If you are sending your news release to several newspapers and stations, it might be best to mimeograph it. If you are sending it to just a couple, you can make carbons. In any event, it's probably best to send the same to all. To prepare individual and different releases for all would be too time-consuming and really unnecessary since each editor will probably have your release rewritten to conform to his style, space, and time requirements.

Such a news release as the one following would have a very good chance of being used by an editor, assuming he had the space or time available. It answers the six basic questions and is presented in logical order.

Logical order to an editor is having the most important news at the beginning and the remaining facts in order of relative decreasing importance.

Trinity Church

18 Elm Street, Millville, New York

NEWS RELEASE

For release: Immediately   Date: May 15, 19—

For further information, contact: Mrs. Vernon Sawyer
1221 Spruce Lane,
Millville, N.Y.
Bellview 4-3185

Trinity Church, Millville, will hold its annual Vacation Church School June 19–30 at the church, 18 Elm St.

Classes will be held Mondays through Fridays for children from kindergarten through sixth grade. Hours will be from 9 A.M. to noon. The school is under the direction of Robert Morris of 1332 Springdale Ave.

On Friday, June 30, at 7:30 P.M., parents will be able to attend a special program prepared by the children enrolled.

Morris said the school is a part of the church's ongoing outreach program and that all local children are invited to enroll whether or not they are affiliated with Trinity Church.

He also pointed out that the dates of the school have been coordinated so as not to conflict with those of similar programs in other churches in the area.

Further information is available by calling Robert Morris at Bellview 4-5376 or the church office, Bellview 4-1050.

#

Compare this news release to the one preceding, both reporting the same event:

Trinity Church

18 Elm Street, Millville, N. Y.

NEWS RELEASE

Robert Morris has agreed to direct our Vacation Church School again this year.

We're all looking forward to the children's program on the closing Friday night. It's always a highlight of each year's VCS for pupils and parents alike.

Many different crafts and activities are planned for this year's school along with an outstanding series of lessons for the children.

Classes will be held each morning for two weeks starting June 19. All children are invited!

#

About the only thing that was done right here is that the "finish mark" (#) was put at the end of the news release to show that there are no subsequent pages!

Mr. Morris's appointment is certainly of interest, but not the most important fact to be related.

And what about the six important questions?

When will the event take place, for instance? Will it be seven days a week? What time will classes begin and end?

Where will the Vacation Church School be held? At the church? At a nearby school? In Mr. Morris's home? And, for that matter, where does he live?

Who can be contacted for further information? Who is affected (what age children are invited)?

How?

Why?

The release would require extensive checking on the editor's part and, if he is hard pressed for time as most are, chances are he wouldn't have time to do this, hence the release possibly would not even be used.

Two other details to note:

— Date your release. The editor will want to know when it was prepared to judge how fresh the news is and, if he decides to file it for future use, whether it will require updating later.

— Give a "release date." You'll note the first example above is marked for "immediate release." This means the editor may use his discretion as to when it should be printed or broadcast. If announcement of an event is planned for a specific date, send the news release in advance and simply mark it for release on the chosen date.

To whom should releases be sent? Phone calls to the newspapers and radio/television stations should provide you with the names of those responsible for church news.

Also, it's best to send the release to every newspaper and station that covers your locality. It probably won't be used in every one, but your chances of at least some publicity are improved by sending it to all.

And, finally, if the story does not lend itself to the listing of a contact person in the story itself, provide one as a note and include a phone number where this person can be reached (see first example above).

Covered News

The media spend most of their time and effort in news work "covering" news events, that is, sending reporters to where the news is happening.

So far, we have been discussing information that you provide for the editor about events or people. There may be occasions, however, when a newspaper or station may be interested in covering an event or meeting involving your church.

If the event is of major community importance (for instance, a housing project involving several churches as sponsors, or the visit of a person of renown beyond just your church or denomination), a news conference might be in order.

A news conference is a meeting of a person or persons having news to impart to reporters. Again, we must take note of the demands placed on an editor's time and on the time of his reporters. It would be well to discuss a news-conference plan with the media in your area to be sure enough of them would be able to be present to make it worthwhile. Like the news release, the news conference should cover the answers to the six basic questions about what is being announced.

If it is a meeting which reporters are invited to cover, encourage the chairman to limit the agenda to the important matters of news value and the members to keep their comments as brief and pertinent as practicable.

News for Radio/Television

Writing for radio and television is an art in itself. The secret, of course, is conciseness and what might be called "audibility."

Material written to be heard on radio and television should be prepared so as to convey as much important information as possible in as short a time span as possible. Short words and short sentences must be used so they can be read aloud and understood easily and clearly.

Since time availability and station style vary so much, it is probably best to send the same news release to the stations as you send to the newspapers. The radio or television editor then will have it written to conform to his needs.

Answering the six basic questions, properly dating your releases, and sending them to all the media serving your locality will virtually assure people will "hear" you

TELLING THE NEWS!

#

7 | Feature News!

Feature news is news which concentrates more on the how and why than on the what and when. That is to say, it is more concerned with the meaning of an event or the background of a person than the regular news story.

It is best to discuss a planned feature with a particular editor in advance. Features generally should not be offered on the kind of blanket basis used for news releases.

Talking with the editor will enable him to guide you as to what he feels would be of most interest to his readership or, in the case of a radio or television station, how a feature story can best be developed for his audience.

Generally, feature news is not in the ordinary news story form. Rather, its opening (known as the lead since it leads off the story) should be interest-catching above all.

Consider the following leads which might be written with the same facts in mind:

Bethel Church held a dinner Friday night. The pastor was the speaker, and Mrs. Emily Scott was honored.

* * *

Emily Scott remembers it like it was yesterday, but the date was May 14, 1898.

* * *

Yes, it's the same story. Although the *what* is certainly told in the first example, in this case it's the *who* that is the story, and that makes it a feature.

Read more of what might appear under the second lead:

That was the day Mrs. Scott was baptized and joined Bethel Church, Millville. And on the seventy-fifth anniversary of that date, last Friday, the church's congregation and numerous visitors gathered at a special testimonial dinner to honor Mrs. Scott.

She is a spry ninety now. She recalled Friday that back in 1898, though, when she was just a young girl, she was "a lot more spry than I am now."

Over 350 persons were at the dinner, including some whose membership in the church goes back over fifty years. But the "star" of the evening was Mrs. Scott, whom many recalled as a longtime teacher in the church school.

"She taught me and she taught my children," said Mrs. Arthur Davis of 139 Mill Road. "She's been an inspiration to so many people."

The church's present pastor, the Reverend Stephen Barnes, welcomed the members, former members, and guests to the dinner held in the church fellowship hall. He then read a testimonial to Mrs. Scott prepared by representatives of the church boards and church school.

In part, the testimonial read:

(etc., etc.)

#

Notice that all six basic questions are answered in the above example. But the emphasis of the story is more on Mrs. Scott as a person than on the event or any current issue.

The feature story might be said to convey feeling more than fact, though the facts are there. It provides depth and insight, a fullness that a straight news story, no matter how complete, does not convey.

It may be on any subject, serious or comical, analytical or lighthearted. The tone sets it apart, and its organization reflects this.

Consider another example of two ways to lead the same story:

The youth fellowship at Trinity Church, Millville, is holding a car wash Saturday on the church parking lot, 18 Elm St.

* * *

Thi Mai isn't lonely any more.

* * *

Again the second example is a feature lead. Reading further under the second lead will explain:

Thi Mai is an eight-year-old Vietnamese orphan. She lives in an orphanage in Saigon, and she wrote recently that she hadn't "a friend in the whole world" until a few months ago.

Now, through the efforts of the Reverend Walter Kern, an American missionary in Vietnam, she has a whole congregation of friends at Trinity Church, Millville, especially the teenagers.

The youth fellowship at the church has unofficially "adopted" Thi Mai as its special concern. This Saturday, the young people will hold a car wash on the church parking lot, 18 Elm St. Proceeds will be sent to Mr. Kern to provide clothing and other essentials for the little girl halfway around the world.

In a letter to the youth fellowship, translated and sent on by Mr. Kern, Thi Mai wrote:

(continues)

#

Again, in this case, the what is told in the first lead. But the story is the *why,* and that makes the facts best suited for treatment as a feature story.

Keep in mind, however, that it is a matter of emphasis. In a feature story, just as in a news story, all six basic questions should be answered.

Generally, features run longer than regular news stories, when comparing the different treatments of the same facts. This is because more attention is given to style of writing and more space is devoted to the details that help give the story its tone.

As can be seen in the examples above, the lead in a feature story does not contain the most important fact as it would in a news story. Sometimes the most important fact is two or three paragraphs into the story.

The feature lead is devoted to an interesting or catchy sentence or two to attract the reader's interest and give the flavor of the story to come.

There are two main pitfalls in writing features. The first is overwriting. Although features will probably be longer than most news stories, they should get to the point fairly quickly and relate only the more essential and interesting details. The problem is that an overwritten story won't keep the readers' interest and, thus, they won't read it, no matter how sound the subject matter.

The second pitfall is wordiness. Because you have more stylistic freedom in writing features, it's easy to get wrapped up in words. When writing about a person, for instance, it's easy to use too many adjectives and too many flowery phrases. In general, keep your expressions simple and direct.

Avoid these pitfalls, answer the six basic questions, and you'll have a feature story that will merit any editor's attention.

As pointed out in earlier chapters, interesting people, events of special significance, and interesting facts about your church or its members or pastor are all worth reporting in the media. These types of subjects, however, lend tnemselves especially well to feature treatment.

Radio and Television Features

Radio and television stations are interested in feature stories, but their needs are much more limited than those of newspapers because of time and format considerations.

It would be best for you to contact the station news editor in advance about a possible feature and discuss with him how he wants to handle its development.

So-called "talk shows," in which a radio or television host or hostess interviews guests, are especially interested in people-centered features.

If an interesting personality is to visit your church, contact stations with talk shows to discuss the possibility of an on-the-air interview with your visitor.

In the case of an unusually interesting project or person in your congregation (like the youth group "adopting" the orphan or the story about Mrs. Scott), a talk-show interview could also be arranged.

Local radio and television stations offer a real opportunity for you to present feature news related to your church.

People are interested in the byways of life just as they are in the main roads of the human course. Providing news in depth and with the color of humanity is important to the media as part of presenting the full spectrum of truth. For these reasons, this type of news should also be of real concern to church news directors.

Then, too, this kind of approach to facts might be an especially relevant one for Christians who realize that importance can often be found more in life's quality than its circumstances.

Be that as it may, editors and church news directors have an important responsibility to provide readers and listeners with

FEATURE NEWS!

#

8 | Pictures and News!

Take a look at the front page of your local newspaper. Note the pictures. Now imagine that page with no pictures at all, just column after column of type. What a gray, unattractive page it would be!

Now leaf through the inside pages of the newspaper. Imagine how those pages would look with no pictures in the news columns and no illustrations in the ads. They'd be pretty dull, wouldn't they?

If you had to make a choice at a newsstand, which would you select: a newspaper with pictures or one without illustration? There's hardly a doubt of the importance of pictures in attracting newspaper readers.

As you watch your favorite television news program this evening, note the number of photographs, filmed reports, and other illustrations employed to help tell the news.

Imagine the telecast without any of these—just the anchor person telling the day's news. It would be difficult to maintain concentration on such a program. Your interest would wane quite soon.

The two examples given above illustrate the importance of pictures in attracting and sustaining the interest of people in what the news media present. And if a news medium cannot attract and sustain interest, the news it presents will not be read or heard.

Certainly words are needed to give the details of the news, but how bare these details would be without some pictures.

News commands both a response of intellect and a response of feeling. It is informational, but it is also a conveyer of emotion.

We are one with other persons in the common human experience. Thus to learn of them and their doings is to feel for them.

Few writers or speakers can match the impact of pictures in conveying the heart of the news.

Recognizing the importance of pictures in telling the news and in making their media products more attractive, editors are constantly on the lookout for good pictures.

You, as your church's news director, can help supply your local editor's needs.

As you perform your duties, developing and assigning stories, writing news releases, interviewing, talking with contact persons, adopt a motto:

THINK PIX!

Go back over the news releases offered as examples in previous chapters of this manual. Think how they might be illustrated.

For instance, building projects (see chapter 1) not only lend themselves to a number of stories, but also can yield a whole series of pictures as planning and construction progresses. These might include:

—Architect's sketch of completed building
—Groundbreaking ceremonies
—Construction progress including, especially, addition of special features (exterior cross, unique furnishings)
—Stained-glass windows (manufacturer can probably provide drawing or photo for reproduction).

All these and more picture possibilities are present. As your building program progresses, THINK PIX!

The announcement of the March Lenten observances (chapter 2) might be illustrated by a picture of the choir (robed and singing, for instance) or one of the "Singing Troubadors." Pictures of the pastor and guest speakers might also accompany the individual releases.

The news release in chapter 3 about church women planning a book sale could be accompanied by a picture of two or three women looking over some donated books. (Note: avoid pictures of people simply staring into the camera; show them in action, since these kinds of pictures are the most interesting and effective.)

Every story about a person (chapter 4) can be illustrated at least by a picture of that person; the best picture would be one of the person doing something related to the story about him or her.

For instance, the story of a new pastor's arrival at a church can be illustrated by a picture of him being greeted by local church or denominational representatives or simply one of him at work in his study.

There are a number of ways you can arrange for pictures to accompany your news release or feature story.

Possibly the most preferable is to arrange for a professional photographer to take one or more pictures of the event or persons involved. Submit these to the editors with the news release or feature story.

Use of a professional photographer will give you both control over the pictures' subject matter and assurance that the pictures will be of high quality.

An equally good and much less expensive method is to have the editor agree to arrange for the photos to be taken by a photographer on his staff. This should be arranged with the editor well in advance because demands on his staff are usually quite heavy.

A third way to get photos is to have a skilled amateur— perhaps yourself or another member of the church—take them. Be sure, however, that he or she can produce the pictures in time for them to be sent out with the news release or for their use by the media. If the pictures are to be developed and printed by a commercial firm, advance arrangements may have to be made to speed up the processing.

A fourth way is to provide the editor with simple snapshots with the news release or feature story. Generally, however, these do not reproduce well for newspaper use. But they are certainly preferable to no pictures at all.

Slides are generally too costly and time-consuming for a newspaper to reproduce, although television stations can often use them more readily. It is always best to check with editors about the acceptability of slides.

Usually editors prefer pictures to be 8″ x 10″ glossy black-and-white prints. Focus should be sharp, and the pictures should have good contrast and be bright enough to assure good reproduction.

As far as the subject matter is concerned, in addition to what has been said, here are a few more guidelines:

—Pictures of inanimate objects (buildings, displays, crafts) are enhanced by the presence of people in action related to the objects.

—Keep the total number of people in a picture to a minimum—four or five is acceptable, two or three is best. Exceptions, of course, are pictures of organized groups like choirs, meeting groups, or groups working or playing together in large numbers. Just remember that when a picture is sized into a newspaper or shown on television, the fewer the number of people, the easier the picture is to view and understand. Simplicity is the key to good news pictures.

—Identify the picture. Provide the editor with complete information about what it shows. Include names and addresses (and ages, if pertinent) of all people pictured, except in the case of large groups. In the latter case, at least identify any people shown who are important to the news involved.

Except in the case of large groups at public gatherings, be sure to obtain the permission of the people shown for use of the picture in the news media. Generally it is best to get this in writing on a form such as the following:

Release

I hereby give permission for photographs taken of me by

_____(photographer)_____ on __(date)__ to be submitted to

_____(news medium)_____ for _____(intended purpose)_____.

_____(signature)_____

_____(date)_____

One other practical point to remember is this: if the pictures are to be used exclusively by the news media and will involve significant expense, it might be well to check with the editors involved as to whether they will be interested in them. In the course of such a discussion, it may also develop that the editor prefers to assign a staff photographer to take the pictures.

Pictures are vital to interesting and complete news coverage. Editors need them to help make their media-products attractive and to maintain reader and viewer interest. As you go about your duties, THINK PIX, remembering that there is no better way to tell a story than through the use of both

PICTURES AND NEWS!

#

Appendix

Your
Church
Newsletter

The church family is just that—a family.

From New Testament times, the people of God have thought of themselves as related in Christ (Galatians 3:26) and referred to each other commonly as brethren and sisters (Romans 12:1; 16:1; 1 Corinthians 1:10; Colossians 1:2; James 2:15).

The other familiar biblical figure by which the church is described is that of a body: "You are the body of Christ," wrote Paul in 1 Corinthians 12:27, "and individually members of it."

And the intimate relationship that should characterize the church fellowship is perhaps best summed up when he says: "We are members one of another" (Ephesians 4:25).

As such, church members care about each other and about the concerns and activities of their common life and work (1 Corinthians 12:12–13:3).

In the church's early days, word of mouth sufficed to keep the members of each Christian group informed about each other. But in today's complex society, in which most church members do not maintain close and regular contact with most others, something more is needed to keep the congregation informed of events and circumstances in the realm of common interest and concern.

News communicated through pastoral visits and letters can help as can notices and announcements in the weekly church bulletin.

But nothing has proved more efficiently effective than a regular church newsletter mailed to the home of each family in the congregation and to those others with whom vital and regular contact is desirable.

The form of the church newsletter varies widely from congregation to congregation, depending on such factors as time, facilities, and money available. What is important, however, is the effort. The simplest of forms can suffice.

There is also a variety of ways in which the church newsletter can be reproduced—from fluid duplication to dry copying—but the most popular, by far, are printing and mimeographing.

The Printed Newsletter

Printing is usually the more expensive of the two popular methods of reproducing the newsletter. Printing costs, like others, are increasing, and most churches cannot afford the outlay, especially when mimeographing offers an attractive alternative at less expense. However, there is little doubt that the well-printed newsletter is attractive and usually easier to read than one that is mimeographed. Such is especially the case if photographs are regularly used. New mimeograph processes do permit quite acceptable photo reproduction, and although this requires special stencils prepared professionally it is still less expensive than printing.

One way some churches offset the high cost of printing is by selling advertising space in the newsletter. Although some churches feel this is not proper, others regularly use paid ads even in mimeographed newsletters to help defray costs.

The Mimeographed Newsletter

Technology has brought mimeographing a long way in recent years. The days of smeared paper and ink-stained hands are virtually gone. Today it is possible to reproduce hundreds of copies by mimeograph which are as clear as the original, with a variety of color inks, attractive lettering and illustrations, and even photographs.

Through the use of specialized stencils, lettering guides, traceable illustrations and instructional guidebooks, anyone with imagination and willingness can produce a very professional-looking mimeographed newsletter.

Information and supplies—and help—are available from mimeograph manufacturers, stationery stores, and many church supply outlets.

Form and Distribution

The church newsletter can be reproduced on both sides of

a single sheet of paper or it can be several sheets. Its sheets may be used full-size or folded to form several pages. White paper, colored paper, or a combination of the two is possible for the newsletter.

In deciding how many sheets or pages to use, give paramount consideration to not crowding any one. White (blank) space helps to set off type and illustrations for easier reading and more attractive layout.

Some church newsletters are sent out in envelopes, while others are folded with address labels attached. The folded variety is often stapled or kept from opening and tearing by the use of a gummed seal or small piece of transparent tape. One point to remember: staples are sometimes difficult to remove without tearing the paper, especially when they hold together several thicknesses of paper. The newsletter editor should check with the local post office to determine the most economical way to mail a newsletter of the size planned.

Although some churches distribute their newsletters at worship services, it is generally best to mail them. That way they are sure to reach the home of every person in the church and church school and the home of each person with whom the church wishes to maintain contact (regular visitors, community leaders, prospective members).

Mailing the newsletter to local editors is also a good idea, but not for the purpose of news releases. Most editors do not have time to scan such newsletters carefully enough to glean all important information.

Content

The content of a successful church newsletter can be divided into five major categories: activities and programs, "people news," the pastor's message, special features, and the church calendar.

Activities and Programs

Upcoming church programs and activities should be described in articles that are brief but complete. Remember the six questions discussed in chapter 6. These six questions should always be answered.

Above each should be a headline—the brighter and more lively, the better. For instance, an article headed "Look What's Happening This Fall!" is much more apt to be read than one titled, "Fall Schedule."

If the church has sports teams, their activities should be reported with names and game descriptions as complete as possible in the space available, and also, where appropriate, team and league records.

Likewise, recent events of note (church meetings, special events, and programs) should be reported.

Some church newsletters carry brief reports of board meetings, noting actions taken and plans considered. These can often serve to encourage wider congregational participation in the church's decision-making process.

The church's stewardship of money is an important matter of concern to all. Many newsletters carry a detailed report of giving on a weekly or monthly basis. Special offerings or needs can also be publicized.

Special services should be given prominent mention, and sermon topics or series may also be announced in advance.

The church newsletter can also be a means of recruitment. "The Church School Needs You!" one newsletter headlined recently. Another included a registration form for vacation church school to be returned to the church office.

All of this attention to the congregation's plans and activities should be balanced by some news of the church's wider family. This would include reports and communications from mission fields, denominational happenings, and the like.

"People News"

The church newsletter should contain a regular feature devoted to news about the people in the church.

Such a feature should probably carry the same headline in each issue. "Personal Notes," "In the Family," "Church Chatter" are examples.

Contained in this article—perhaps one long paragraph with a sentence or two devoted to each person mentioned with dots separating subjects—would be notes about honors, unusual experiences, vacations, births, or family visitors. Each name should be set off from the rest of the sentence by capitalization or underlining to make the paragraph easier on the eye of the reader.

Separate attention should be given to those in the hospital, those bereaved, and new members. Separate notice might also be given to changes of address and notifications of departing members.

Another article might list birthdays for the period covered by the newsletter. This may be located anywhere in the newsletter but might best be placed on the calendar page for easy reference. Some churches also list wedding anniversaries in this way.

The Pastor's Message

Except in the smallest churches, it would be impossible for the pastor to visit each church family as frequently as a newsletter can be published.

Some pastors use the church newsletter to provide each reader with a devotional message or sermonette. Others comment on church activities, needs, and concerns. Still others offer personal reflections on a variety of subjects. Many vary their purpose from issue to issue.

To whatever end, the pastor should be provided space in each issue to communicate with the church family. His article may have a formal title, such as "From the Pastor's Study," or an informal title, such as, in the case of one church, "Joe's Jottings."

Special Features

Public recognition of service is an expression of gratitude used by many churches. Aside from such recognition at worship services or meetings, the newsletter can be a means of saying "Thank you" to members of the congregation.

Expressions of appreciation from members who have been served by the church or its people in a special way (visits, cards, help in need) may also be included in the newsletter.

Some church newsletters provide Bible study aids and suggestions for daily devotional reading, perhaps selecting a "Bible Book of the Month."

Some also mention new books available for borrowing in the church library or from the pastor, along with capsule reviews. Again, a headline like "Book Nook" or "The Bookshelf" is more inviting than one like "New Library Acquisitions."

Also in the realm of special features are foreign-language articles or sections which some churches provide where the community has a sizable foreign-language-speaking group within it.

Occasionally, the attention of the newsletter's editor will be drawn to a passage, quotation, poem, or cartoon in another publication which he or she feels should be included in the newsletter. In such a case, that person should be sure to secure permission from the copyright holder before reproducing the material.

The Calendar

For the convenience of readers, the newsletter should contain some type of calendar to cover the period until the next publication date. This may be a chronological listing of important dates or a regular calendar sheet with activities noted in "day blocks."

One church annually provides each family with a special backing sheet to be hung on a wall. The top of the sheet contains the church name, address, and phone number along with similar data on pastor and key staff members as well as times of regular services. With each month's newsletter a calendar sheet is provided for affixing to the bottom of the backing, thus making an attractive wall calendar.

Be sure to include the time that each event is to take place with the listing on the calendar.

Naming the Newsletter

As with so many other aspects of newsletter production, imagination is the key to naming it. Some churches run a contest among members or youngsters in the church school both to get a name and to generate interest in the newsletter.

Some names are based on alliteration ("Trinity Times," "Bethel Beacon"); others have theological implications ("The Witness," "Tidings").

Whatever name is chosen, that name, along with the church name and address and date of publication, should be designed into a "masthead" or "flag" which should appear at the top of the first page of the newsletter much like that of a newspaper.

Either as part of the flag or at a separate location, each issue should contain the names of the pastor, key church staff members, and the newsletter editor. Phone numbers for these might also be provided to facilitate contacts in connection with activites described in the newsletter.

The editor may also wish to mention the time by which he or she must receive material for inclusion in the next newsletter and where it is to be delivered.

Preparing the Newsletter

Generally, a church newsletter needs a basic staff of at least two persons, although its tasks can be combined in smaller churches. These are the editor and the typist.

If the newsletter is not to be printed, one of the two should be familiar with such jobs as stencil preparation and the operation of necessary equipment. Instruction in such subjects is available from supply dealers and manufacturers.

News can be secured for the newsletter using the same network of contact persons assigned by the news director to supply information for news releases to the media (see chapter 5). The pastor can often be helpful in providing leads on "people news," but, no matter the source, the editor of the newsletter should always check with the persons involved before using their names.

Working cooperatively, the church news director and the editor of the church newsletter can be of invaluable assistance to one another in turning up news and seeing to its appropriate dissemination.

Layout and Design

Generally, the front page of the newsletter should carry

the most important news, although many churches reserve this space for the pastor's message.

If possible, place regular features ("people news," birthday list, Bible study) in the same location in each issue. Regular readers will appreciate knowing where to look for those features in which they are especially interested.

With the possible exception of the church calendar and the pastor's message, it is usually best to divide each page into two columns. The editor should not be concerned with the typist making an even margin on the right; this is just too time-consuming unless a specially equipped typewriter is being used.

Use of illustrations, headlines in a variety of sizes, and white (blank) space to advantage will make each page attractive and assure that the reader will not face a forbidding jumble of type.

Most articles may be single-spaced and should be freely paragraphed. Double-spacing or use of italics is acceptable for variety, but use this technique sparingly. If each article looks too different, the page will appear confusing.

The editor should set up deadlines with contributors (contact persons, pastor) which are well enough in advance so that time can be spent on article preparation and experimentation with layout.

"If one member suffers, all suffer together; if one member is honored, all rejoice together. Now you are the body of Christ and individually members of it" (1 Corinthians 12:26-27).

Being informed of one another's joys and sorrows and of our common task as the family of God is a responsibility of church membership. Facilitating this interpersonal contact is the unique opportunity of those who produce

YOUR CHURCH NEWSLETTER.

#